Green Rl

by
Audrey Greaves

Published by Quacks Books
Petergate, York YO1 2HT

British Library Cataloguing in Publication Data
Greaves, Audrey 1994
Green Rhythm
Great Britain

ISBN NUMBER 0 948333 34 0

Obtainable from :

39 Moss Street
York YO2 1BR
or ring : 0284 705035

Price £3.50 plus post and packing

vi,46pp

Printed by Quacks Printers, 7 Grape Lane, Petergate, York, YO1 2HU

I am a visual artist and lyrical poet.

In my paintings form takes marginal precedence over colour.
The poems are personal without being confessional.

The theme of my work is the interdependence of all living things encompassing birth, love, motherhood nature and death.

I am a vegetarian and work as a part-time R.G.N.
Currently doing black and white drawings,writing, illustrating and painting.

Audrey Greaves
21 April 1994

CONTENTS

PART I

Dream

My room
In dream
I hover and peer
Through empty eye-sockets
Pretend
I'm pretending
Waiting to pounce
Push back the wall
I cannot get in.

Night Thoughts

Some days
It seems quite probable
You will walk
Into my room
Your absence
But a space
Between
The flower's bud and bloom.

Meanwhile
I play the guessing game.
Will you
Won't you
Will you
Release our joyful feet
And make
Peels of magic laughter
Waken me
From sleep?

Full Moon

There is
A full moon tonight
With strips of cloud
Across it
Slowly weaving.

You are not here
To feel the cold, sharp air,
To touch again
The magic
Of that evening.

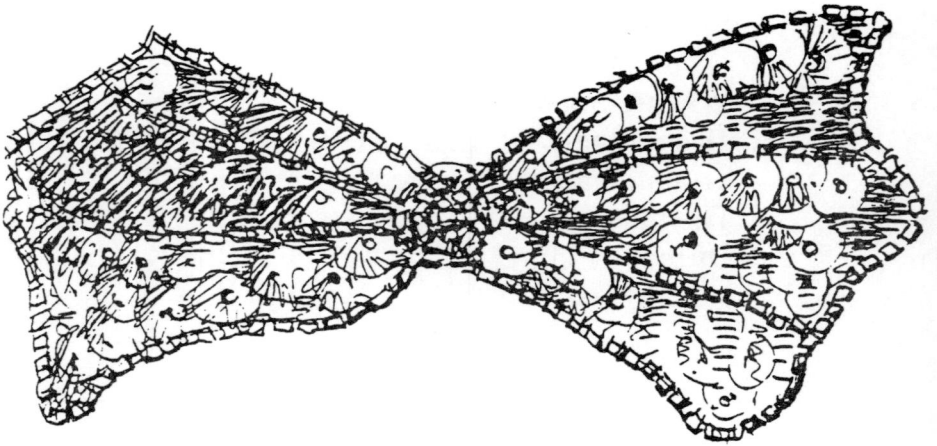

A Death

She leaned her head
Against my side
And gently cried.
The innocent knowledge
In her eyes
Which I denied
Remained with her
Until she died.

Light Touch

She came
She went
No epitaph set up
Few remember
The girl
Who would have been
The woman.

She came
And went,
A fitful breeze
On a summer's day
She made no mark
But in the breath
Of passing.

The Spot

The mattress
With the stain
Haunts my waking dreams,
The spot
Where your dear head
Had briefly rested.
That place
From which I hid
And shut myself away
Not to face
The image
You had pressed there.

Now
I call it all to mind
The pain
Is never less
Than in the space
You did not take another breath.
With your dark hair
Spread about
Warm upon my arms
And I held you
As the waxen pallor crept.

Inside
I cried
"Don't leave me"
But there was no reply
And I laid you
By my side
Upon the bed.

7

Wound

The world
Just fell apart
One day

From bliss
To emptiness.

A clean sharp break
Is best they say
But, the edges are like knives
My fingers are all cut about
I cannot staunch the stream
Of blood
That flows
From deep inside.

Advent

Suddenly
The gold is gone
Red leaves rustle
Underfoot
Naked branches
Inter-twine
Along the wall
A rime of frost
Crystal
Bright
And knife-sharp cold
This first day
Of my winter.

Autumn

Autumn falls
Winter calls
Leaves wither on the bough
Spring has gone
And in between
One long sun.
Where is that summer now?

PART II   DEEP ROOT

Hope

First there was hope.
Hope for the starlight
Hope for the moon-glow
The touching of hands
And toes
In the sand
Of a blossoming desert
Finding a rose.

Deep Root

Why do I keep falling
Falling
Down
Black holes?

Grey day
Winter day
Why so sad?
Spring is coming

New is young
Young is tender
All must die
That is sad.

Who looks ahead?

The cat sits on the mat
The woman rocks the cradle.

Free song
In the sky
Fall light
Butterfly

Deep root
In the mind
Velvet room
Ruling deep

No sound
Underground
In this country
Iron bones

Spilling through
Above the roar
Torrents pour
Love.

Rock, rock, rock, the cradle
Sit, cat, on the mat.

Black Holes

Round and round
I walk
In my black hole
Waiting
For some light to fall.

Beware
I am about to jump
From nothing
Into nothingness.

Don't try
To tranquilize me
That
Would destroy
Reality
Or kill me
Before the darkness
Is dissolved.

October's Day

White
White is the light
Over wet rooves
Spreading.
A dark
Flat disc
Obliterates the sun
Squeezing red
From its edges
One probing shaft
Stabs
Through the sky
A bird flies past.
October's day
Has ended.

First Fall

In the night
It came.

Those lovely heads
That yesterday
Were lifted high
In glorious salutation
To a cloudless sky
Are now
Bowed down
Brought low
Relentlessly adorned
With snow.

Summer Passing

You did not see my garden
When it wore
It's summer crown.
Now all the garlands are faded
And every leaf is brown.

But a child walks
In my garden
Though his footsteps make no sound
The echo of his young song
Fills all the air around.

Partition

I am
The property of those
I love and yet
My own.

This self
Divided
In the end
Is whole.

From scene
To scene, wholeness
Inviolate
Moves on.

A gift
Complete, it gives
Retracts and leaves
It's soul

Yet does not feel
The lack
Upon reflection still
Is whole.

Commute
Commiserate
Participate, give all, remain
Intact.

PART III

Bramble Wood

Today
I pricked my finger
And
The taste of blood
Was sweet.

The scent
Of all worlds flowers
Poured
Through that slit
In the skin

The essence
Of early life's spices
Perfume
Of pine-sap and fir
Blue twisting whiskers of wood smoke
And berries
Pungent
As May on its bough.

I know
This flow
Is not mortal
It springs
From the rocks and the seas

Sulphurous vapours
Of heaven
And music
From far away fields

Distilled
Into channels
And rivers
Veins
For the forming
Of words.

This
I knew
On the day
That I wandered
Into a bramble-bound wood

Red Sandals

The lamps were few
And far between
The stars then shone
For me alone.

I moved beyond
The speed of light
From the garden gate
To the bridge
At the end of the road.

In the blinking of an eye
I had the whole world seen
And come back again
Red sandals
On the road.

24

Asthmatic Child

The candle flame is flickering
While I fight for breath.
Why do you keep arguing
When all I want is air?

The incense still is burning
Blue smoke round me curling
In this chapel
Laid aside
On my back
I silent cry
From my cot.

(I am four And should be in a little bed)

"Daddy, daddy, come to me
For I cannot breathe you see
And the shadows on the wall
They frighten me."

"Please, mummy, love me
Mummy mummy love me
Four years is not so long
And you are *very* strong."

"Oh, Mummy
Daddy
Stop it."

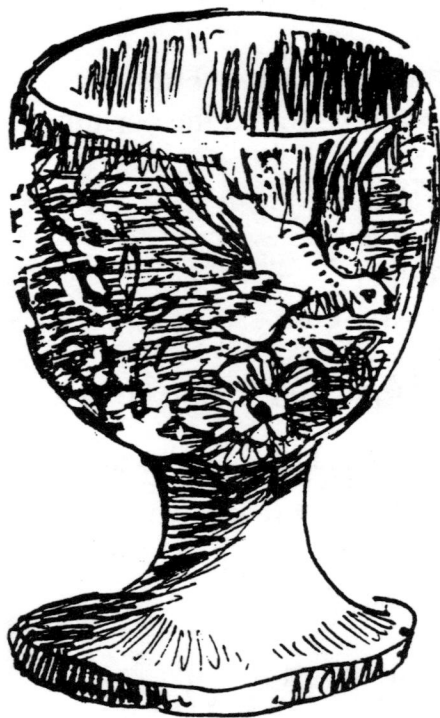

Sunshine Home

Red sandals
In the lamplight
Red sandals
Through the grass
Scarlet
On the bed-sheets
Beside
The empty box.
Small feet
Warm feet
Sliding
Into cold
Hurry, do the buckles up.
Cover up
Red feet
Go to sleep
Dream sweet
Daddy's child.

An Apple for the Pony

The ring of blows on iron
Sizzling in a trough of steam
Places long lived in
Cottages and country lanes.

An apple for the pony
Black paint for Mary's hooves
Bright and shining
Sprightly prancing
Haughty, wilful
Long mane dancing
Grandfather's darling.

Sweet Sixteen

I am
The receptacle
For your incompatibility.
The battle continues
Over my head
Increasing the pain
In my virginal flow.

You grow
Old in your war.
Too long
Have I been
Under your spell.

I cannot stay longer
In this zone.

I must go.

Down to the Sea

Give me your hand
And I will lead you
To where
The wavelets
Wash along the shore
Past the babies play
And the little running stream
To where
The ocean rolls and groans
Curls its foam
And hurls
Its torrent
Round your feet.

Legacy

This legacy
I give you
Gathered from the years
Your heritage.

A Norfolk beach

The shingle rolls
Along the line of sand
Startling cold.
Like stones
Blue-eyed children stand.

A Hampshire lane

Soft and green
Primroses growing
In the quiet earth
A hazel copse
And bluebells.

An idyll but

Intrusion
Of a sloe-black mood
Disturbs the wood.
You will not travel easy
With this mixture in your blood.

PART IV

Spring Bud

Along the branches
Little buds
Like pointed candles
Stand
Slow exploding
Into white
Grow tall
And shiver
Schooled for growth
By April's wilful weather.

Blue Jelly

Today
I made a jelly
Blue
Bright and gleaming
A see-through sea
Of aquamarine.

What fruit did I use?
I cannot remember.

It was made of a dream.

Lily Song (ii)

The lilies
Are in bloom again.
Night
Has turned aside its face
And scatters gold
Into the world
With brief
Abandoned radiance.

Green Rhythm

I like to be
Enclosed in green
Green and deep
Deep and green

Far from
World entanglement
Or sapping joys
Of sharing

A noiseless place
Where thoughts flow free
And surging blood
Seeks newness in retreat

This green pulse beat
Is steady
Measured
Deep.

Mermaid

Long creamy body
Pink standing nipples
A mermaid
In water
Elbows pointed
Finger-tips touching
Sloping thighs
And narrowed feet.

I am dissolving
Floating away

Back into dream
Rocked by waves
Of a fathomless sea
In a hammock of bubbles
Bearing me bright
As a treasure
Trailing with jewels
Culled from the crest
Of a frivolous tide.

Live For Ever

Far and deep
My mind has ranged
To find that inner world
An order In the heart of things
Outside of space
And time.

Other boys
Will hold the rain *
And other girls
Blow kisses
And make music
To indifferent passers-by
While
This green summer lasts.

* From The Telling of Days

The Merman's Child

From the sea
You came.
Those little feet
At home in water
Or on land
Through all the green wet grass
Ran
To the very edge

Stood poised
An emeral deep before
Stretched out,
Then sprang

The only indication
Of your flight
A rippling line
Of light.

Shell Path

When I stepped out
On the lonely road
It was
Good-bye to you
And you
And you.

Under the bridge
The water flowed
High overhead
The clouds were blown
Good-bye
Good-bye.

An image
Has no thick or thin
No bevelled glass
To see itself in

So I lay out a path
Of delicate shells
Whitened by tides
Of the shifting sand
And placed by feet
One by one
On the fragile line
To carry me over

Carry me over.

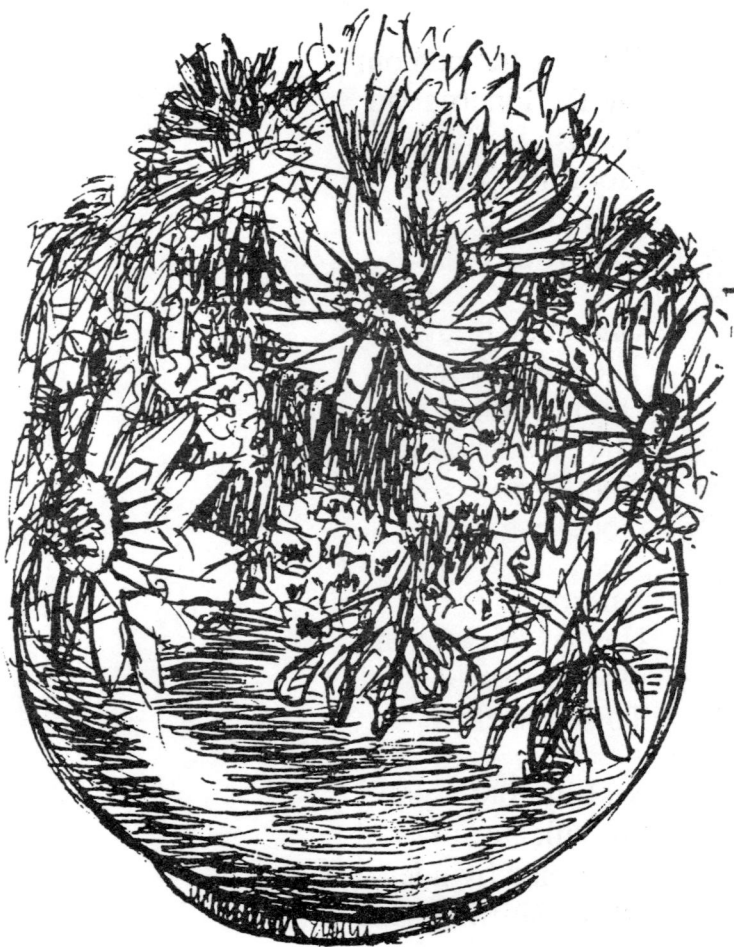

Sun Dance

The sun
A golden ball
Descends

On your eye-lids
Speckling violet
Falls
From lilac skies

And all the while
You slowly smile

We dance

And weave
Our ring of green.

Stone, Fire and Water

My song is a bird
Wide-winged and strong
My song is the bridge
We are travelling along.

Stars in the sky
Lift my song up high
And down on the ground
The round smooth stone
That curves to your arch
Is the one of all others
Your foot lights upon.

Under the bridge
A river runs cool
Its surfacing ripples
Are playing the fool.

My song is a fire
Fierce-burning and bright
That scatters the darkness
And lights up the night.

By earth, fire and water
The music moves on
This song has no end
The singing is all.

Most recent work by the same author *The Telling of Days,* a book of illustrated poems.

Both *Green Rhythm and The Telling of Days* are available to purchase on cassette, readings with music.

My aim :-

'…to express a sincere human feeling'

Vincent van Gogh

'Existence is hardly interesting save on the days when the dust of realities is shot with magic sand.'

Marcel Proust